Instant
Send-Home Letters

50 Reproducible Letters
That Help Build Essential Literacy Skills
and the School-Home Connection

BY JOAN NOVELLI

SCHOLASTIC
PROFESSIONAL BOOKS

NEW YORK • TORONTO • LONDON • AUCKLAND • SYDNEY
MEXICO CITY • NEW DELHI • HONG KONG

Thanks to Jackie Clarke for her careful reading of the manuscript and for her thoughtful and enthusiastic feedback.

☆ CREDITS ☆

"Monsters" from *Monster Hotel* by Douglas Florian. Copyright © 1993 by Douglas Florian. Reprinted by permission of Harcourt Brace.

Read Together! Multilingual Tips and Bookmarks adapted from *Read Together: A Multilingual Guide to Getting Parents Involved* (Scholastic, 1998). Translations provided by Linguistic Systems, Inc.

Produced by Joan Novelli
Cover design by Norma Ortiz
Interior design by Kathy Massaro
Interior art by James Graham Hale

ISBN 0-439-10618-4
Copyright © 2000 by Joan Novelli.
Printed in the U.S.A.

Contents

About This Book

*H*ow can I help my child become a better reader? Is it okay to let my child spell words incorrectly? Why does my child ask so many questions? What kinds of answers should I give? What is the best way to help my child with homework? How can I improve my child's math skills? What are some ways to help my child become a good person? These are just some of the questions parents ask as they try to understand the best ways to help their children learn and grow. Research supports parents' involvement in their children's education—not only in the ways they help at school, but also in the ways they can reinforce skills and concepts at home. Research also shows that what parents most want to know about helping their children achieve in school is how they can help at home.

This collection of reproducible send-home letters is designed to help you guide parents in supporting their children's academic, social, and emotional growth at home. From mini-notes that make it easy for your students to share the day's events with their families, to informative letters that include strategies and activities for strengthening skills across the curriculum, the reproducibles in this book will help you build the school-home connections that help students succeed.

School-Home Connections Letter

When you're ready to send home your first Instant Send-Home Letter, attach a copy of the introductory letter on page 8. You may also adapt the information in this letter to create your own.

Mini-Notes

Keep copies of these pages (9–10) handy for notifying families about conferences, homework, and other news.

Read Together!

What languages do your students and their families speak? Spanish? Polish? Korean? Cambodian? Others? A special section on reading at home appears in ten different languages to help you communicate with parents whose first language is not English. (See pages 17–26.) Each reproducible includes suggestions for reading with children plus a bookmark with more helpful hints. Though the other send-home notes in this book appear in English only, you may want to invite members of your community to help out by translating some or all of the pages into the languages spoken by your students' families. Look for multilingual volunteers among your school's parents and staff, students and staff at local universities or colleges, and local businesses.

"Ask Me About My Day" Mini-Notes

Ask a child, "What did you do in school today?" and the response, regardless of the day's events, is likely to be, "Nothing." These reproducible notes encourage conversation about school, and can be customized to let families know about whatever's going on: assemblies, special visitors and events, science experiments, stories, math activities, and more. Make a class set of the pages, cut them apart, and store them in large, recloseable sandwich bags for easy access. You can let children select these notes on their own when they have something they want to share at home, or you may choose occasions to give them to the entire class. In either case, be sure to allow time for children to fill in the blanks and draw pictures as indicated.

"Ask Me About My Week" and "Weekly News"

These reproducible notes help you keep families up to date and encourage conversations about school at home. "Ask Me About My Week" makes it easy to share classroom news and gives parents and other family members lots of leads for starting conversations about school. (See page 13.) The "Weekly News" is a more traditional class newsletter that lets you share highlights, reminders, and so on. (See page 14.)

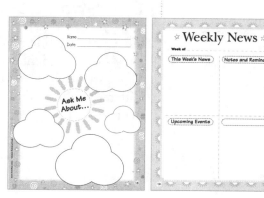

Language Arts Send-Home Letters

Assorted pages guide families in supporting literacy at home. There are tips on choosing children's books, strategies for supporting beginning readers and writers, listening games, and more.

Math Send-Home Letters

These pages cover counting, number sense, estimation, measurement, fractions, money, time, patterns, shapes, and more. Suggestions include easy-to-do games, investigations, and activities built around everyday experiences.

Science Send-Home Letters

In addition to notes you can customize to share information about in-class experiments, investigations, and so on, you'll find tips and activities for helping families reinforce process skills such as observing, classifying, and communicating at home. Suggestions are built around everyday family activities.

Social Studies Send-Home Letters

These pages guide families in helping children explore their homes, neighborhoods, communities, and the larger world. In the process, children can learn about different cultures and develop understandings in geography, history, and basic economics.

☆ Teaming Up With Technology ☆

In addition to using the send-home letters in this book, you may want to consider the ways a classroom computer can help you build strong school-home connections.

E-Mail Updates E-mail is an efficient way to communicate with families. Anyone with a computer, modem, and phone line can send and receive e-mail messages in seconds. No more waiting for a phone at school, leaving messages, or playing phone tag. If you've got information that pertains to the entire class—for example, a reminder about a field trip or suggestions for supporting reading at home—you can type in one message and forward it to everyone with just a click. It's easy to send individual messages, too, letting you share information about children's accomplishments and needs on a day-to-day basis.

Class Web Site Make your classroom part of the World Wide Web's resources by creating a class web site. In doing so, you'll give families one more way to support learning at home. You can showcase student work on the web site, post homework assignments, share activities, offer links to family-friendly sites, and more. There are many ways to go about creating a class web site. The best place to start is with your building or district technology coordinator. For a detailed look at how some schools created web sites, see *Kids Do the Web* by Cynthia Bix (Adobe Press, 1996).

To Learn More

For more information on involving families in students' learning and development, you may find the following resources helpful.

◎ *Building Successful Partnerships: A Guide for Developing Parent and Family Involvement Programs* by the National PTA (National Education Service, 2000). This practical guide includes a section on involving families in student learning. To order, call (800) 733-6786 or go to **www.nesonline.com**.

◎ **Center on School, Family and Community Partnerships.** Current projects include development of the National Network of Partnership Schools, which works to build school, family, and community partnerships. For related research and publications, go to **www.csos.jhu.edu**. For more information, call (410) 516-8818 or e-mail **nnps @ csos.jhu.edu**.

◎ **The National PTA.** Programs include Building Successful Partnerships, designed to help schools increase parental involvement. For more information, go to **www.pta.org**; e-mail **info@pta.org**; or call (800) 307-4PTA.

Dear _____ ,

If you've ever wondered what you can do at home to best support your child's education, you're not alone. Research shows that what parents most often want to know about helping their children succeed in school is how they can help them at home.

Throughout this year, your child will be bringing home letters and mini-notes that are designed to help you learn more about what's happening at school and guide you in strengthening important skills and concepts. You might like to store these notes in a folder or binder so that you can easily revisit the activities with your child throughout the year.

The first Send-Home Letter is attached. Please let me know if you have any questions or comments about this or any of the other Send-Home Letters you receive. I'm looking forward to working with you in an effort to help your child learn and grow.

Sincerely,

_____

Your Child's Teacher

Date _____

☆ Thank you! ☆

Dear _____ ,

_____

_____

_____

Sincerely,

_____

Your Child's Teacher

- -

Date _____

☆ Conference Reminder ☆

Dear _____ ,

_____

_____

_____

Sincerely,

_____

Your Child's Teacher

Date _____

☆ Homework News ☆

Dear _____ ,

_____

_____

_____

Sincerely,

_____

Your Child's Teacher

- -

Date _____

☆ We Need Your Help! ☆

Dear _____ ,

_____

_____

_____

Sincerely,

_____

Your Child's Teacher

Name _____

Date _____

Ask Me About My Day

I did something special today! Ask me about it!

I drew a picture about my day.

- -

Name _____

Date _____

Ask Me About My Day

I had an extra-great day at school! Ask me about it!

Here's a picture about my day.

Name _____

Date _____

Ask Me About My Day

We had a special visitor today. Ask me about our visit!

Here's a picture about our visit.

Name _____

Date _____

Ask Me About My Day

We went on a field trip today. Ask me about it!

Here's a picture about the field trip.

Name _____

Date _____

Ask Me
About...

Weekly News ☆

Week of ....

This Week's News

Notes and Reminders

Upcoming Events

Homework Helpers

Dear _____ ,

Does your child misplace assignments, leave things until the last minute, or resist sitting down to do homework? Your child's homework is important for several reasons. Homework is a way to strengthen and extend skills and concepts learned in school. Experience with homework at the primary grades can also help your child develop good study habits for the upper grades, when assignments may become more demanding. Learning to handle homework can help your child become more organized and efficient, a plus in just about any area of life. To help your child succeed with homework, consider these tips.

- Help your child set up a study space. Your child may have his or her own desk. A corner of a counter and a box for holding materials will also do. The key is to make it easy for your child to find necessary books, papers, and so on.

- Help your child schedule a time each day for homework. Right after school may not be the best time, as your child may need to relax a bit. After dinner may be too close to bedtime. A good time might be during dinner preparations, when an adult is nearby to offer support.

- Use a timer to help your child set goals and concentrate. For example, set the timer for 15 minutes. When the buzzer goes off, let your child stretch before setting the timer again. Adjust the time to meet your child's needs.

- Allow your child to ask for help. Sometimes assignments that make sense during school are unclear hours later at home. Ask your child to explain what he or she can about the assignment, then do your best to fill in the blanks. Breaking up assignments into smaller chunks may also help.

- Plan a treat that your child can look forward to when homework is finished—for example, a story you read with your child or a game you play together.

Sincerely,

_____

Your Child's Teacher

Copy and cut out these mini-notes. Punch a hole at the top and string with yarn. Children can wear these notes home to announce literacy news!

I read a great book today!
Ask me to tell you more.

☆ Title ☆

_____

_____

I read a great book today!
Ask me to tell you more.

☆ Title ☆

_____

_____

Read Together. Your Child Will Love It!

Show Your Child That Reading is Important to You...

💜 Make sure your child sees you reading. No matter what you like to read—newspapers, magazines, romance novels, comic books—it is important that your child knows that you enjoy reading, too.

💜 Keep books, magazines, and newspapers around the house.

💜 Read in any language. If you don't read in English, don't worry. Read to your child in the language you're most comfortable with! What's important is that your child sees that you enjoy reading together.

💜 Take children's books with you wherever you go: to the doctor, to the market, on the bus, anywhere. Restless children love having a book to keep them busy.

💜 Let your child have his own special place to keep his books— a shelf, a milk crate, or a corner of a bookshelf.

💜 Encourage your child to sit with a book, to look at and talk about the pictures, or just to pretend she is reading.

READ TOGETHER. Your Child Will Love It!

To get the most out of reading with your child, try these suggestions:

● Put your child on your lap and look at the book together.

● Don't worry about reading every word.

● Turn the pages slowly and encourage your child to talk about the pictures.

● Make reading together a special time for you and your child— every day!

Lean juntos.
¡A su hijo le encantará!

Muéstrele a su hijo o hija que la lectura es importante para usted...

❤ Asegúrese de que su hijo o hija la vea leyendo. No importa qué le guste leer a usted—periódicos, revistas, novelas románticas, tiras cómicas—es importante que su hijo o hija sepa que a usted también le gusta leer.

❤ Tenga siempre libros, revistas y periódicos en la casa.

❤ Lea en cualquier idioma. Si usted no lee inglés, no se preocupe. ¡Léale a su hijo o hija en el idioma en el que se sienta más a gusto! Lo importante es que el niño o la niña vea que a usted le encanta cuando leen juntos.

❤ Lleve libros infantiles a cualquier lugar que vayan: al doctor, al supermercado, en el autobús, a todas partes. A los niños inquietos les encanta tener un libro para entretenerse.

❤ Permita que su hijo o hija tenga su propio lugar especial para guardar sus libros—un estante, una caja o la esquina de un librero.

❤ Anime a su hijo o hija a sentarse con un libro, mirar la imágenes y comentarlas, o simplemente hacer como si leyera.

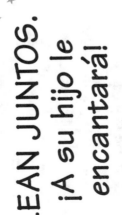

LEAN JUNTOS. ¡A su hijo le encantará!

Para aprovechar al máximo la lectura, siga una de estas sugerencias, o todas ellas:

● Siente al niño en su regazo y vean el libro juntos.

● No se preocupe por leer cada palabra.

● Voltee las páginas lentamente y anime a su hijo o hija a hablar sobre las imágenes.

● Aparte una hora especial para leer con su hijo o hija —¡diariamente!

Lisez ensemble. Votre enfant adorera ça!

Montrez à votre enfant que vous aimez lire...

❤ Assurez-vous que votre enfant vous voit lire, peu importe ce que c'est: journaux, revues, romans, bandes dessinées. Il est important qu'il sache que vous aussi, vous aimez lire.

❤ Gardez des journaux, revues, livres en évidence dans la maison.

❤ Lisez dans différentes langues. Si vous ne lisez pas anglais, ne vous inquiétez pas. Lisez à votre enfant dans la langue avec laquelle vous vous exprimez le mieux. L'essentiel est que vous appréciez tous deux ces moments de lecture.

❤ Emmenez des livres d'enfants partout où vous allez, par exemple chez le médecin, au supermarché, dans l'autobus, etc. Les enfants impatients aiment avoir un livre pour les occuper.

❤ Laissez votre enfant garder ses livres dans un endroit spécial: une étagère, un casier ou un compartiment personnel.

❤ Encouragez votre enfant à s'asseoir avec un livre, à le regarder et à commenter les images; ou simplement prétendre lire.

LISEZ ENSEMBLE. Votre enfant adorera ça!

Pour tirer le plus de profit de vos lectures partagées, essayez ces suggestions:

● Prenez votre enfant sur vos genoux et feuilletez le livre ensemble.

● Ne vous forcez pas à lire tous les mots.

● Tournez les pages lentement. Encouragez votre enfant à commenter les images.

● Mettez de côté quelques minutes pour lire avec votre enfant. Tous les jours!

和孩子一起讀書，您的孩子一定會喜歡！

讓孩子知道讀書對您是何等重要...

❤ 務必讓您的孩子看到您在讀書。無論您喜歡讀什麼－報紙、雜誌、小說、連環圖畫書－要緊的是要讓您的孩子知道您喜愛讀書。

❤ 在家裡各處都擺放書籍、雜誌和報紙。

❤ 讀任何語言的書都可以。如果您不識英文，那沒有關係。您可以用您最熟悉的語言朗讀 給您的孩子聽。要緊的是讓您的孩子知道您喜愛與孩子一起讀書。

❤ 去哪兒都應該帶著兒童圖書：去看病，去超級市場、乘車，等等。好動的兒童閑不住，有了圖書就可以使他們有事可做。

❤ 讓孩子有自己專門的地方放書－擱板、紙板箱或書架的一個角。

❤ 鼓勵孩子隨時帶著一本書，有時間就看看或談談圖畫；或者只要求孩子裝作在讀書的樣子。

和孩子一起讀書，您的孩子一定會喜歡！

如想達到和孩子一起讀書的最佳效果，不如試下列部分或全部的建議：

● 讓孩子坐在您的膝蓋上一起讀書。

● 不必要讀出每個字，您可以以增添或刪掉一些東西以便使故事更有趣。

● 翻書的速度要要慢，鼓勵您的孩子看圖講故事。

● 每天撥出一段特別的時間和孩子一起讀書！

함께 읽으세요.
아이가 무척 좋아할 것입니다!

읽는것이 당신에게 중요하다는 것을 자녀에게 보이십시오...

당신께서 읽는 것을 자녀가 꼭 보게 하십시오. 신문, 잡지, 연애 소설, 만화책, 당신께서 그 무엇을 읽기를 좋아하시든지 상관없으며, 중요한 것은 귀하께서 읽기를 좋아한다는 것을 자녀가 아는 것입니다.

책, 잡지, 신문을 집안 주위에 놔두십시오.

어떤 언어로든지 읽으십시오. 영어로 읽지 못하셔도 상관없습니다. 사용하시기에 가장 편한 언어로 자녀에게 읽어주십시오! 중요한 것은 당신께서 함께 읽기를 즐겨한다는 것을 자녀가 보게끔 한다는 것입니다.

의사에게 가거나, 시장을 보러 가거나, 버스 안에서나, 어디를 가시든지 자녀의 책을 가져가십시오. 아이들은 가만히 있지 못하기 마련이어서, 책으로 자신을 바쁘게 하기를 좋아합니다.

선반, 우유 운반상자 또는 책꽂이의 한 모퉁이와 같이, 자녀가 자신의 책을 보관할 특별한 장소를 마련해 주십시오.

자녀가 책을 갖고 앉거나, 그림을 보거나 그에 관해 이야기하거나, 읽는 시늉만이라도 하게끔 격려하십시오.

함께 읽으세요. 아이가 무척 좋아할 것입니다!

함께 읽는 시간으로부터 처음부터 끝까지 즐거운 읽기 위해, 다음 제안을 명심하십시오:

- 자녀를 두 팔에 앉히고 책을 함께 보세요.

- 단어들을 일일이 다 읽어야 한다고 걱정하지 마십시오.

- 페이지를 천천히 넘기면서 자녀가 그림에 대해 이야기 하게끔 격려하십시오.

- 함께 읽는 것을 귀하와 자녀가 날마다 특별히 여기는 시간으로 삼되, 매일 그렇게 하십시오!

អានរួមគ្នា។ កូនលោកអ្នកនឹងស្រឡាញ់ចូលចិត្តាជាមិនខាន!

បង្ហាញកូនអ្នកឲ្យដឹងថាការអានមានសារៈសំខាន់ណាស់សម្រាប់អ្នក...

♥ ធ្វើយ៉ាងណាឲ្យកូនអ្នកមើលឃើញ ថាអ្នកកំពុងអាន។ ទោះបីជាអ្នកចូលចិត្តអានអ្វីៗ ដូចជាសារពត៌មាន ទស្សនាវដ្ដី ប្រលោមលោកសៀវភៅកំប្លែង ក៏ដោយ ក៏ជាការសំខាន់ដែរចំពោះកូនអ្នក នៅពេលដែលគេឃើញថា អ្នកមានភាពសប្បាយរីករាយក្នុងការអាន។

♥ ឲ្យមានសៀវភៅ ទស្សនាវដ្ដី និងសារពត៌មានគ្រប់ទីកន្លែងនៅក្នុងគេហដ្ឋាន។

♥ អានក្នុងភាសាណា ក៏បានដែរ។ បើមិនអាចអានភាសាអង់គ្លេសបានទេក៏មិនអីដែរ។ អ្នកអាចអានភាសាណា ដែលអ្នកចេះហើយចូលចិត្តវា! អ្វីដែលសំខាន់គឺចង់ឲ្យកូនអ្នកមើលឃើញ ថាអ្នកពិតជាចូលចិត្តអានរួមមែន។

♥ ទៅទិណា ក៏ដោយត្រូវយកសៀវភៅរបស់កូនទៅជាមួយដែរ ឧទាហរណ៍ ដូចជាទៅ ផ្សារបណ្ណិត ផ្សារ ជិះរថយន្តក្រុង ឬកន្លែងផ្សេងៗ។ ក្នុងចូលចិត្តឲ្យខ្លួនគេ រាល់ជាមួយនឹងសៀវភៅណាស់។

♥ អនុញ្ញាតិកូនអ្នក ឲ្យមានកន្លែងពិសេសសម្រាប់ទុកសៀវភៅ ដូចជា ធ្វើ ទ្បាំងសម្រាប់ដាក់ទឹកដោះគោ ឬ ជ្រុងនៃធ្នើដាក់សៀវភៅជាដើម។

♥ លើកទឹកចិត្តកូនអ្នកឲ្យអង្គុយដោយមានសៀវភៅនៅជាមួយ ហើយឲ្យក្រឡេកមើល និងពណ៌នាអំពីរូបភាពទាំងឡាយ ឬក់ត្រានៅតែក្នុងធ្វើជាដោយឧបមាថាគេកំពុងតែអានសៀវភៅប៉ុណ្ណោះ។

Đọc Sách Cùng Nhau. Con Em Quí Vị Sẽ Yêu Thích Việc Đọc Sách!

Hãy Cho Con Em Quí Vị Thấy Rằng Việc Đọc Sách Là Quan Trọng Đối Với Quí Vị...

❤ Hãy chắc chắn rằng con em quí vị thấy quí vị đọc sách. Bất luận quí vị thích đọc những gì -- báo, tạp chí, tiểu thuyết, sách hài hước -- điều quan trọng là con em quí vị biết rằng quí vị rất thích đọc sách.

❤ Hãy giữ nhiều sách, tạp chí, và báo trong nhà.

❤ Hãy đọc bằng bất cứ ngôn ngữ nào. Nếu quí vị không đọc bằng tiếng Anh cũng đừng ngại. Hãy đọc sách cho con em quí vị nghe bằng bất cứ ngôn ngữ nào quí vị thấy dễ dàng nhất! Điều quan trọng là con em quí vị thấy rằng quí vị thích đọc sách cùng các em.

❤ Hãy đem theo những sách chuyện dành cho trẻ em với quí vị bất cứ quí vị đi đâu: tới phòng mạch bác sĩ, đi siêu thị, trên xe buýt, bất cứ nơi nào. Những trẻ em hiếu động rất thích có một cuốn sách để các em có thể bận rộn.

❤ Hãy để con em quí vị có nơi đặc biệt riêng để giữ sách của các em -- một kệ, một thùng đựng hộp sữa hay một góc của giá sách.

❤ Hãy khuyến khích con em quí vị ngồi xuống với một cuốn sách, xem và nói về những hình ảnh; hay chỉ giả vờ đang đọc sách.

Đọc Sách Cùng Nhau. Con Em Quí Vị Sẽ Yêu Thích Việc Đọc Sách!

Để có được nhiều kết quả nhất từ việc đọc sách cùng con em quí vị, hãy cố thử áp dụng một số hay tất cả những đề nghị sau đây:

● Đặt con em lên lòng mình và xem cuốn sách chuyện cùng nhau.

● Đừng cố gắng đọc tất cả mọi từ.

● Hãy lật qua những trang một cách chậm chạp và khuyến khích con em quí vị nói về những hình ảnh trong đó.

● Hãy khiến việc đọc sách cùng nhau là một thời gian đặc biệt cho quí vị và con em quí vị-- hàng ngày!

اقرأوا معاً،
فذلك يفرح ولدكم!

أبدوا لأولادكم الأهمية التي تعطونها للقراءة ...

♥ احرصوا على أن يراكم ولدكم تقرأون. مهما يطيب لكم قراءته ـ الصحف أو المجلات أو الروايات العاطفية أو الكتب الهزلية الكاريكاتورية ـ فلا بد لولدكم أن يدرك أنكم تستمتعون بالقراءة مثله.

♥ احفظوا الكتب والمجلات والصحف في أنحاء المنزل.

♥ اقرأوا في أي لغة. لا تقلقوا إذا كنتم تجهلون القراءة بالإنكليزية، بل اقرأوا لولدكم باللغة التي تحسنونها وترتاحون إليها! المهم هو أن يدرك ولدكم أنكم تستمتعون في القراءة معه.

♥ خذوا معكم كتب الأولاد حيثما ذهبتم: إلى عيادة الطبيب، إلى السوق، في الباص، في كل مكان. فالأولاد المتململون يفرحون لوجود كتاب يلهيهم ويشغل ذهنهم.

♥ دعوا الولد يحتل مكاناً خاصاً يحفظ فيه كتبه فيه ـ رف خاص به، أو صندوق، أو زاوية في رف الكتب لديكم.

♥ حثوا ولدكم على الجلوس وكتابه في يديه يتطلع فيه ويتكلم عن صوره؛ أو دعوه يتظاهر بأنه يقرأ.

اقرأوا معاً، فذلك يفرح ولدكم!

• اجعلوا من القراءة معاً مناسبة خاصة ـ في وقتٍ يوم.

• تمهلوا في قلب الصفحات وحثوا ولدكم على أن تقرأوا النص بحذافيره.

• لا تشعروا أنه من الضروري أن تقرأوا النص بحذافيره.

• اجلسوا وولدكم في حضنك وانظروا إلى الكتاب معاً.

• هذه الأقلام حجة، جربوا بعض هذه النشاطات من القراءة حجة، جربوا بعض للاستمتاعة من القراءة معاً.

Читайте вместе!
Ваш ребенок будет это любить!

Дайте понять своему ребенку, какое важное значение имеет для Вас чтение

- ❤ Позаботьтесь, чтобы ребенок видел, как Вы читаете. Не имеет значения что Вы любите читать — газеты, журналы, романтические новеллы или комиксы — важно, чтобы Ваш ребенок знал, что Вы тоже получаете удовольствие от чтения.

- ❤ Разложите книги, журналы и газеты по всему дому.

- ❤ Читайте на любом языке. Если Вы не умеете читать по-английски — ничего страшного. Читайте своему ребенку на том языке, который Вы знаете! Самое главное — показать ребенку, что Вам нравится читать вместе с ним.

- ❤ Всегда берите детские книжки с собой, куда бы Вы ни шли: к врачу, в магазин, чтобы почитать в автобусе, куда угодно. Детям трудно усидеть на месте, и они любят иметь книжки под рукой, чтобы чем-то заняться.

- ❤ Отведите ребенку его собственное место, где он мог бы держать свои книжки: полку, коробку или угол книжного шкафа.

- ❤ Побуждайте своего ребенка сидеть с книжкой, просматривать и обсуждать картинки или просто делать вид, что он ее читает.

Читайте вместе! Ваш ребенок будет это любить!

Чтобы получить как можно больше пользы от совместного чтения, попробуйте некоторые, а то и все, из следующих рекомендаций:

- Возьмите своего ребенка на колени и вместе просматривайте книгу.

- Не старайтесь прочесть каждое слово.

- Переворачивайте страницы медленно и побуждайте ребенка обсуждать картинки, которые он видит.

- Сделайте из совместного чтения особое занятие, которым Вы занимаетесь с ребенком каждый день!

Czytajcie razem ku uciesze Twojego Dziecka!

Pokaż dziecku, że czytanie ma dla ciebie duże znaczenie

❤ Zwróć uwagę by Twoje dziecko widziało jak Czytasz. Bez względu na to co lubisz czytać– gazety, czasopisma, romanse czy komiksy – ważne jest, by Twoje dziecko wiedziało, że Ty też lubisz czytać.

❤ Trzymaj w domu dużo książek, czasopism i gazet.

❤ Czytaj w takim języku, który ci odpowiada. Jeśli nie umiesz czytać po anigelsku, nie przejmuj się tym. Czytaj swojemu dziecku w takim języku, którym najlepiej się posługujesz! Najważniejsze jest bowiem to, by Twoje dziecko wiedziało, że lubisz z nim czytać.

❤ Wszędzie gdzie idziecie, zabieraj książki dla dzieci: do lekarza, do sklepu, do autobusu, wszędzie. Aktywne dzieci bardzo lubią zajmować się książkami.

❤ Pozwól dziecku, aby miało swoje własne specjalne miejsce na swoje książki – półkę, pudło czy też róg w regale.

❤ Zachęcaj dziecko do siadania z książką, patrzenia na obrazki i opowiadania o nich, czy choćby udawania, że czyta.

Czytajcie razem ku uciesze Twojego Dziecka!

W celu osiągnięcia najlepszych rezultatów przy wspólnym czytaniu, wypróbuj niektóre bądź wszystkie poniższe propozycje:

● Weź dziecko na kolana i razem oglądajcie książkę.

● Czytanie każdego słowa po kolei nie jest najważniejsze.

● Kartki przewracaj powoli i zachęcaj dziecko, by opowiadało o obrazkach.

● Organizuj czas na czytanie ze swoim dzieckiem— codziennie!

When You Read to Your Child

Dear _Parents_,

The road to raising readers starts long before your child acquires reading skills. It begins with those first stories you read to your child. Reading aloud is important for many reasons. It introduces language skills to your child, helping to develop sound-letter relationships and an understanding of the structure and grammar of sentences. Experts recommend that you continue reading aloud with your child even after he or she is reading independently. This time spent together will nurture your child's love of reading and provide the support he or she needs to grow as a lifelong reader. Here are some tips for reading with your child.

- Set aside a regular time to read together. For many families, that's bedtime. Be sure to give your child plenty of time to get ready so that neither of you feels rushed. Plan to read for about 20 minutes at a time. More than this and your child may get restless.

- Involve your child in choosing books to read. Don't be afraid to stop reading a book if it is not holding your child's attention.

- If you can't complete the story in one sitting, find a suitable place to stop, such as the end of a chapter.

- Remember that your child can enjoy read alouds that he or she is not yet ready to read independently. An older child will also enjoy picture books.

- Children love it when you substitute their names for those of characters in a book. Use simple props to help set the scene, too. For example, turn off the lights and use a flashlight when reading a mystery.

- Weave poetry into your read alouds. Rhythm and rhyme have great appeal to children, who enjoy chiming in on predictable words.

- Take the advice of Carolyn Feller Bauer, author of *This Way to Books* (Wilson, 1983): "Remember your flood book." Take a book along whenever you go anywhere. You never know when you might have a few minutes to enjoy a story or poem together!

Sincerely,

Mrs. Saxon

Your Child's Teacher

When Your Child Reads to You

Dear _____Parents_____,

When you listen to your child read aloud, you may wonder what to do if he or she comes to an unknown word. Here are some strategies to support and encourage your child while reading.

◎ If your child attempts to sound out an unknown word, don't immediately say the word. Give your child some time to put those skills he or she is learning to work.

◎ If your child asks for help with an unknown word, say the word and let your child continue reading. Asking your child to sound out the word may interrupt his or her understanding of the meaning of the story, which is the goal of reading.

◎ If your child substitutes one word for another, for example, says "flower" instead of "marigold," don't stop to correct the mistake. A substitution such as this does not interfere with the meaning of what is read.

◎ Let your child know how much you enjoy his or her reading. Your enthusiasm and attention will fuel your child's interest in learning to read.

Sincerely,

Mrs. Sayon

Your Child's Teacher

Tip

Alphabet and counting books provide great success for beginning readers, who enjoy reading them again and again. A few favorite titles follow.

Clifford's ABC by Norman Bridwell (Scholastic, 1983). Busy illustrations invite young readers to identify pictures for each letter of the alphabet.

Dr. Seuss's ABC by Dr. Seuss (Random House, 1963). "Big A, little a, What begins with A? Aunt Annie's alligator...A...a...A." You can sing this ABC book to the tune of the alphabet song. Read it often, inviting your child to substitute his or her own words for each letter.

Eating the Alphabet by Lois Ehlert (Harcourt Brace, 1989). Fruits and vegetables come to life in this colorful book. Plan a snack in honor of your child's favorite letter. How about blueberries, bananas, and bagels for the letter *b*?

Choosing Books for Your Child

Dear _____,

"How do I choose the best books for my child?" The children's section of a library or bookstore can be overwhelming. Here are some tips that can make the selection process easier—and help you take home books that will continue to motivate your young reader.

1 What are your child's interests? Is he or she currently fascinated by trucks, bugs, or princes and princesses? Look for books that connect with those interests.

2 Keep the classics in mind. Some of the books you loved as a child may be just as appealing now.

3 Take note of books your child seems to enjoy. Look for books by the same author or illustrator. These people will become like old friends to your child.

4 If your child likes fairy tales, look for different retellings of a favorite.

5 If your child is a beginning reader, select some books with repeated text. These books will help your child read along with you or more easily read the text on his or her own. An example is Eric Carle's *The Very Hungry Caterpillar* (Putnam, 1981).

6 Consider award-winning titles, such as Caldecotts (the best illustrations of the year) and Newberys (best story of the year). These books, such as the Caldecott winner *Make Way for Ducklings* by Robert McCluskey (Viking, 1941), often endure over time, and may appeal to your child as much as they have to countless other children.

7 For more ideas, check with your school or public library media specialist. Or investigate reading resources on the Internet. One favorite is Carol Hurst's Children's Literature Site (**www.carolhurst.com**), an extensive site that includes reviews of children's books.

8 Most importantly, involve your child in choosing books to read. Children are often drawn to books adults may overlook.

Sincerely,

_____

Your Child's Teacher

Books for Beginning Readers

Dear _____,

If your child is a beginning reader, you may struggle to find books that are just right for him or her to read independently. "Predictable books," named for features that assist beginning readers, are a good choice. The attached page lists some predictable books you might enjoy reading with your child. Features of predictable books include:

- a repeated sentence or phrase, such as "Is your mama a llama?" in the book by the same name by Deborah Guarino (Scholastic, 1989).
- a cumulative pattern in which a sentence is repeated as the story builds.
- pictures that help tell the story.

Try these activities to build success into your child's reading experiences.

Read With Me

Sign out a few predictable books from the local or school library. As you read them with your child, invite him or her to chime in on the predictable text. Share these books again and again to build your child's confidence in reading.

"I Can" Books

Help your child make a predictable book. Staple blank paper together. Let your child make a cover. Include the title and author's name (your child). On page one, write the following sentence starter: "I can _____." Have your child fill in the blank. Have your child complete this sentence on each new page. Invite your child to read the finished book to you. For new books, just change the sentence beginning. For example, you might start with "My cat _____." Or, borrow a pattern from a book you and your child read together and create your own version of the book.

I can swing.

Sincerely,

_____

Your Child's Teacher

Books for Beginning Readers

Try these titles to encourage your beginning reader. Each has built-in features to help your young child grow as an independent reader. Some have repeated text. Others have rhyming patterns, familiar story lines, or helpful pictures.

1 *Do You Know How Much I Love You?* by Donna Tedesco (Bradbury, 1994). This will be a bedtime favorite. Your child will delight in reading it to you, too!

2 *Eating the Alphabet* by Lois Ehlert (Harcourt Brace, 1989). Pictures of fruits and vegetables for each letter of the alphabet make this a good choice for beginning readers.

3 *Fox in Sox* by Dr. Seuss (Random House, 1965). Any of the Seuss books will have your child rhyming and reading.

4 *Guess What?* by Pam Ayers (Knopf, 1987). Picture clues invite young readers to tell what characters in the story will do.

5 *Have You Seen My Cat?* by Eric Carle (Scholastic, 1987). The title of the book repeats in the story, as a boy looks for his missing cat.

6 *The Important Book* by Margaret Wise Brown (HarperCollins, 1949). What is important about a spoon, a shoe, or the sky? Find out in this book, by the author of *Goodnight Moon*. Repetitive text makes it easy for young children to read along. An affirming message awaits readers at the end.

7 *I Went Walking* by Sue Williams (Harcourt Brace, 1990). Take a walk with the boy in this story. What will you see? Repetitive and rhyming text, as well as pictures, help your child find out.

8 *Piggies* by Audrey Wood (Harcourt Brace, 1991). Ten lively little piggies move from fingers to toes in this whimsical bedtime book.

9 *Polar Bear, Polar Bear, What Do You Hear?* by Bill Martin (Henry Holt, 1991). It's always fun to fill in the animal sounds in this book. Try *Brown Bear, Brown Bear, What Do You See?*, too.

10 *Time for Bed* by Mem Fox (Harcourt Brace, 1993). Pictures of parent and baby animals help children read this story.

Adapted from Getting the Most from Predictable Books: Strategies and Activities for Teaching with More than 75 Favorite Children's Books *by Michael F. Opitz (Scholastic Professional Books, 1995).*

Building Basic Reading Skills

Dear ___Parents___,

Your child's ability to recognize word parts (for example, syllables and sounds) is called *phonemic awareness*. Strengthening phonemic awareness will help your child develop reading skills. It will also help your child learn to spell words. Here are some games you can play with your child to develop phonemic awareness.

Clap the Beats

RO - BER - TO!

Clap the syllables in your child's name as you say it. Ask: *How many claps do you hear in your name?* Ask your child to clap your name. Listen for the "beats." Now invite your child to clap the beats in words that have the same number of syllables as his or her name. Listen again for the number of "beats" in each.

Sounds the Same

Say your child's name, stretching out the beginning sound—for example, *Sssssarita* (*Sarita*). Have your child say a word that has the same beginning sound (such as *silly*). Continue, taking turns saying words with that beginning sound until you can't think of any more or you run out of time.

Make a Rhyme

Does your child's name have rhyming potential? (For example, if your child's name is *Will*, you can rhyme it with *dill, Jill, mill, drill, grill*, and so on.) Take turns saying words that rhyme with your child's name. You can allow silly words, too, which will make it easier to work with names that are hard to rhyme. If it's too difficult to rhyme your child's name, choose a word for something around you, such as *chair* (*hair, care, bear, wear, air, fair, pear*). At this point, don't be concerned that the rhyming parts have the same spelling. Concentrate on letting your child hear sounds that are the same.

Sincerely,

Mrs. Saxon

Your Child's Teacher

Connecting Sounds and Letters

Dear _Parents_,

Making connections between letters and sounds is one of the strategies children rely on for reading unfamiliar words. Your child is learning the sounds that individual letters make (such as the letter -*b* in *boy*), the sounds that blended letters make (such as -*sn* in *snake*), and the sounds that word families make (such as the -*ake* in *snake*). Here are some games you and your child can play to practice these reading skills.

Letters on Labels

Play a game looking for letters on packaged foods. For example, if you've got a jar of grape jelly, ask your child to find a capital *G*. Then see if your child can read the word *Grape*. Your child may use a combination of clues, including pictures on the can, to read the word.

Initials in the News

Give your child the front page of the newspaper. Ask your child to find five words that start with the same letter as his or her first name. Read these words together. Ask your child to listen for the way they sound the same (beginning letter sound). Try names for other family members—even a pet if you have one.

Looking for Little Words

Play a game with letters on labels, cereal boxes, game boards, and so on. Start by looking at a word together. What little words can you find within this word? For example, you can see the word *cook* in *cookies*. Say the little and big words aloud. Listen to the way the letters sound.

Sincerely,

Mrs. Saxon

Your Child's Teacher

Word Families Build Reading Skills

Dear _____Parents_____,

Bat, hat, sat, cat...how many words can your child make with the /at/ sound? A series of letters that stands for a certain sound—such as the /at/ in *bat*—is called a *phonogram* or *word family*. Learning the sounds that phonograms make can help children read unfamiliar words. You can strengthen your child's word recognition skills, reading fluency, and even spelling skills by working with word families.

Play a Rhyming Game

Think of an easily rhymed word, such as *stick*. (In this case, the word family is /ick/.) Take turns naming words that rhyme with this word, such as *pick, quick, sick, kick, lick*. Play until you've run out of words to rhyme. Then pick a new word and play again.

Build a Word Ladder

At the bottom of a sheet of paper, in large letters, write a simple rhyming word, such as *cat*. Above this word, write ___ *a t*. Invite your child to fill in the first letter to make a new word, such as *bat*. Above this word, have your child write ___ *a t*. This time, you fill in a letter to make another new word, such as *hat*. Continue taking turns until you reach the top of the page or run out of words. Read the words in your word ladder together. Then have your child read them to you.

r a t
m a t
h a t
p a t
s a t
b a t
c a t

What's the Word?

Reading rhyming poems with your child is a fun way to practice word families. Start with a poem such as "The Monster Chef," which appears on the attached page. Read the poem aloud to your child. Then read it again, line by line, letting your child fill in rhyming words. Don't worry if your child's word doesn't match the word in the poem. Just have fun playing with the words!

Sincerely,

Mrs. Saxon

Your Child's Teacher

Word Families

The Monster Chef

The monster chef cooked up a meal
Of spotted toad and speckled eel.
He threw some socks into a pot
And boiled buttons piping hot.

He slowly simmered rubber hose
And steamed a lizard's pointed nose.
He griddled a fiddle and baked a rake
Then stuffed a statue in a cake.

He poached a roach and grilled a drill
Then smoked a broken windowsill.
He fried a frame and broiled a broom—
I think I'll stay inside my room.

—Douglas Florian

Try This!

Play a rhyming game with your child. Choose a word at the end of a line in the poem, such as *rake* or *room*. Take turns saying words that rhyme.

"The Monster Chef" from *Monster Motel* by Douglas Florian. Copyright © 1993 by Doug Florian. Used by permission of Harcourt Brace.

Words to Know

Dear _____,

Words like *it* and *the* are examples of words that children encounter often as they read. For this reason, it is helpful for children to recognize these words quickly—without stopping to sound them out. Attached is a set of word cards for some of these words. You can help your child learn them with these activities.

Old Friends, New Friends

Cut apart the word cards on the attached pages. Store the cards in an envelope labeled "New Friends." Label another envelope "Old Friends." Go through the set of words, placing the card for each word your child already knows by sight in the "Old Friends" envelope. Practice the new words for a few minutes each day. Have your child add cards for words he or she learns to the "Old Friends" envelope. Watch it grow!

How Many in a Minute?

Ask your child how many of the words he or she can read in a minute. Ready, set, go! Whether or not your child meets his or her prediction, praise your child for the words he or she can read or attempts to read. You can keep a graph to watch that number grow over time. With practice, your child will recognize more and more of these words on sight.

I Spy an Old Friend

Encourage your child to notice when he or she sees any of the words on the list. For example, your child may spot them as you read a story together or see them on a sign. Making connections like these will reinforce your child's recognition of these words.

Sincerely,

_____

Your Child's Teacher

NOTE: The words on the attached cards are the 150 most frequently used words according to the *American Heritage Word Frequency Book*, as reported in *Phonics From A to Z* by Wiley Blevins (Scholastic Professional Books, 1998).

Words to Know

the	but	into	long	also
of	what	has	little	around
and	all	more	very	another
a	were	her	after	came
to	when	two	words	come
in	we	like	called	work
is	there	him	just	three
you	can	see	where	word
that	an	time	most	must
it	your	could	know	because
he	which	no	get	does
for	their	make	through	part
was	said	than	back	even
on	if	first	much	place
are	do	been	before	well

Words to Know

as	will	its	go	such
with	each	who	good	here
his	about	now	new	take
they	how	people	write	why
at	up	my	our	things
be	out	made	used	help
this	them	over	me	put
from	then	did	man	years
I	she	down	too	different
have	many	only	any	away
or	some	way	day	again
by	so	find	same	off
one	these	use	right	went
had	would	may	look	old
not	other	water	think	number

Letters Make News

Dear ___Parents___,

Simple letter recognition games can help your child become familiar with print and build fluency in reading. Use a newspaper to play the games here. Newspapers give children experience with real-life reading, and also provide examples of print in different shapes and sizes.

I Spy Letters

Look at a newspaper with your child. Have your child notice the different ways letters are used—for example, in headlines, in captions, in stories, to tell who wrote a story, and so on. Take turns asking each other to find certain letters, for example a capital *B*, a lowercase *a*, a *b* next to an *l*, a word ending in *at*, and so on. To start, stick with letters in headlines. These letters are usually big and will be easier for your child to see.

Give Me a B!

Children are often confused by letters with similar shapes, such as *b* and *d*, *p* and *g*, *m* and *n*, *w* and *v*. Using headlines on a page of the newspaper, ask your child to find the letter *b*. How many can your child find? Your child will have fun using a highlighter or light-colored felt tip pen to mark the letters. Continue, this time looking for the letter *d*. One trick you can share with your child is that a little *b* goes the same way as a big *B*. Play the game with other letters, too.

Letter Cutouts

Give your child a pair of children's scissors and a page or two of the newspaper. Have your child cut out letters that match the letters in his or her name. Let your child glue the letters on paper to spell his or her name—as many times as there are letters!

 Tip

You can also play games like these at a restaurant, having your child look for letters on the menu. It's a fun way to pass the time while you wait for your order.

Sincerely,

Mrs. Saxon

Your Child's Teacher

Books and Beyond

Dear _____,

Wondering what to read with your child? Books, of course. But try these other reading materials, too. You'll help your child discover the many reasons people read every day!

Read...

Labels
Recipes
Menus
Catalogs
Cereal boxes
Greeting cards
Flyers
Signs
Numbers on clocks, houses, stores,
    and more
Game directions
Maps
Phone messages
Phone books
Color names on crayons
Web pages
CD-ROM user manuals
Letters
E-mail messages
Coupons
Calendars
Currency
License plates
Truck lettering
Grocery lists
Bumper stickers

What other things can your child find to read? List them here.

_____
_____
_____
_____
_____
_____
_____
_____
_____
_____
_____
_____

Sincerely,

_____
Your Child's Teacher

Tell Me a Story

Dear _Parents_,

Children love to retell stories they've heard or read. Retelling stories strengthens many reading skills, including summarizing, sequencing, and identifying the main idea. You can help your child develop these skills by retelling stories at home. Following are two strategies for helping your child retell stories.

Somebody...Wanted...But...So

Stories often follow this four-part structure: *Somebody* (main character) *Wanted* (what the character wants) *But* (what keeps the character from getting what he or she wants) *So* (how the character overcomes the problem). Recognizing this structure can help your child make sense of a story. It is also a useful activity for helping your child learn to summarize what he or she has read, without including every detail. After reading a story together, or having your child read one to you, ask your child to retell it. Use the clue words *somebody, wanted, but,* and *so* to guide your child's retelling.

First...Next...Then...Finally

This structure guides children in retelling a story in sequence. Recognizing the sequence of events in a story helps your child understand a story and improves comprehension. After reading a story together, or having your child read one to you, ask your child to retell the story. Remind your child to tell what happens in order. Use the clue words *first, next, then,* and *finally* to guide your child.

Sincerely,

Mrs. Saxon

Your Child's Teacher

What's It All About?

Dear _____,

Identifying the main idea of a piece of text is a skill your child will continue to strengthen throughout the elementary grades and beyond. While children are often able to recall every detail of a story, it can be difficult for them to determine the most important information. Learning to recognize the main idea will help your child sort through information to better comprehend what he or she reads. Here are some ways you can work with your child to strengthen this skill.

The Big Picture

Let your child select an interesting picture in a newspaper or magazine. Ask your child: *What is this picture about?* For example, if the photo shows a baseball player sliding into home plate, your child might say the photo is about baseball. Help your child differentiate between a main idea and details by stating the main idea, then taking turns naming details in the photo.

Skip the Details

After sharing a story (fiction) with your child, ask: *What do you think the story was about?* Though your child may want to give every detail, encourage him or her to stick to the big idea. For example, after reading *Owen* by Kevin Henkes (Greenwillow, 1993), your child might say the story is about a boy (mouse) who doesn't want to give up his baby blanket.

Sincerely,

_____

Your Child's Teacher

Sequencing Skills

Dear _____ ,

Understanding the sequence of events in a story helps your child make sense of what he or she reads. *Sequence* is the order in which things happen. It's a skill your child will use in many areas of life—for example, to give or follow directions. Following are activities for strengthening sequencing skills.

Story Strips

Use your child's own stories as reading material. Write down a story your child tells. Start each sentence on a new line. Cut apart the story, sentence by sentence. Mix up the sentence strips and let your child put them back in order.

I played with Damian at recess.
We played tag.
We played until we were out of breath.
Jake and Tucker played too.

Comic Strip Cut-Ups

Read a comic strip together. Cut it apart into single frames. Challenge your child to put them in order. Your child may use picture clues as an aid in sequencing the frames.

Rebuilding a Recipe

Write a simple recipe on an index card, one direction per line. Read the recipe aloud, then cut it apart, step by step. Mix up the steps and ask your child to put the recipe back together from beginning to end. If possible, follow your child's rebuilt recipe to check the sequence. For a twist, invite your child to give directions for making a favorite food, such as a peanut butter and jelly sandwich. List the steps on paper as your child dictates them. Try out the recipe!

Sincerely,

_____

Your Child's Teacher

Strengthening Spelling

Dear _Parents_,

I lk to pla skr. (I like to play soccer.)

Young children go through phases as spellers, including one in which they use letters they hear to write. As children become more aware of the letters that represent sounds, their spelling becomes more recognizable. Learning rules and patterns will help your child become a stronger speller, too. Here are some tips for guiding your child's spelling efforts at home.

About Invented Spelling

Invented spelling (also called *developmental* or *temporary* spelling) is when your child uses the letters he or she hears to spell words. For example, if your child hears the *l* and *k* in *like*, he or she may spell it *lk*. With time, practice, and guidance, your child will use conventional spelling more frequently. In the meantime, using invented spelling allows your child to write much more than he or she could if correct spelling was expected. Writing, in turn, provides real reasons to learn to spell! Encourage your child's progress in spelling by providing opportunities for writing at home. For example:

- Let your child make a grocery list. Write the conventional spelling of each item underneath.
- Make mini-books from photos. Let your child write captions for the pictures.
- Involve your child in writing to relatives and family friends.

Play Word Games!

Playing word games with your child will reinforce conventional spelling. Board games such as Scrabble Junior™ and Boggle Junior™ are wonderful spelling strengtheners. You can make up your own games, too. Here's one you can play again and again, wherever you are.

1. Write a simple word on a piece of paper—for example, *fun*.

2. Let your child change one letter to make a new word—for example, *fan*.

3. Continue, taking turns changing a letter to make new words.

Sincerely,

Mrs. Saxon

Your Child's Teacher

Write to Spell

Dear _____,

Studies link writing to spelling: The more children write, the stronger their spelling will be. Look to everyday life for meaningful reasons to write: grocery lists, phone messages, and more. Include your child in these activities to strengthen writing skills—including spelling. Ideas follow.

> Shopping List
> milk
> eggs
> carrots
> joose
> penut butter
> noodles
> flower
> blueberries
> goop

◎ Post a pad of paper and pencil on the refrigerator. (You can purchase pads with magnetic strips on the back or use a magnetic clip.) When you run out of something, such as milk or juice, invite your child to write it on the list. Encourage your child to read the items on the list as it grows.

◎ Let your child record upcoming events, such as play dates, birthdays, and school vacations, on a calendar.

◎ If you need to take a phone message, let your child write it down. Check to make sure important information is legible.

◎ Cut up sturdy paper into notecard-size pieces. Invite your child to decorate them with designs and pictures. Have your child use the cards to write thank-you notes for gifts, visits, and so on.

◎ If you have e-mail access at home, involve your child in corresponding this way with a family friend or relative. (Be sure to review safety rules for Internet use.)

◎ Let your child help fill out order forms—for example, filling in such things as name and address.

◎ Encourage your child to put his or her birthday wish list in writing.

◎ If you're planning a party, let your child write the guest list, and help with invitations or place cards.

Tip

If your child asks how to spell a word, you might have him or her give it a try, then help out. Keep the focus on writing.

Sincerely,

_____

Your Child's Teacher

Listening Games

Dear _____,

How many times have you heard your child say "What?" when you asked him or her a question? Listening is a skill that your child can strengthen with practice. Play these games to help your child tune in.

All in a Row

Make a game out of helping your child clean up. Start by naming one thing to pick up, then two, three, and so on. How many items can your child listen for and remember in a row?

What Doesn't Belong?

Name an assortment of items, all but one related in some way—for example, _orange, grape, banana, sneaker, mango_. Can your child tell the one that doesn't belong?

Simon Says

This familiar game is always a favorite. To play, face your child and give commands to follow, such as "Simon says, 'hop on one foot,'" or "Simon says, 'swing your arms in a circle.'" Your child should follow the commands that start with "Simon says." If you give a command that does not start with "Simon says," such as "touch your knees," your child should ignore it. Play until your child follows a command by mistake that does not start with "Simon says." Then trade places and let your child test _your_ listening skills!

Sincerely,

_____

Your Child's Teacher

Name _____

Date _____

Ask Me About Math

In math today, I solved a problem. Ask me to tell you more.

Here's a picture that shows what I learned.

Name _____ Date _____

Ask Me About Math

I took a survey about _____ in school today.

I'm going to take a survey at home, too.
My survey question is

_____.

Ask me to tell you what I find out.

Name _____

Date _____

Ask Me About Math

I learned about measuring in math today. Ask me to show you how I can measure things at home.

Here's a picture of me measuring.

- -

Name _____

Date _____

Ask Me About Math

I can skip count by

_____.

Ask me to show you!

Here's a picture of something I counted.

Count Them Up

Dear ___Parents___,

Number concepts in the early grades include identifying quantities (how much) and discovering relationships between numbers. For example, your child might be able to count five toes on each foot for a total of ten, and come to understand that ten is the same as five, two times. (This experience with counting lays a foundation for later experiences with multiplication.) You can strengthen your child's understanding of math concepts with these counting activities. Encourage your child to share reasoning along the way, telling you not only what the answer is, but how he or she got it.

Eyes and Ears, Fingers and Toes

Ask: *How many eyes are there in our family? Ears? Hands? Feet?* (This is a good chance for your child to count by twos and discover that as each person's eyes/ears are counted, the number doubles.) To practice counting by fives or tens, do fingers and toes.

Doorknob Math

Invite your child to guess and then find out how many doorknobs there are in your home. Your child may count each one, or count doors, then double the number (figuring that there is a doorknob on each side of the door). Go further by counting legs on chairs, panes in windows, and so on.

Count Around the Room

Find a pile of something for your child to count—books on a shelf, stuffed animals in a basket, pennies in a jar, apples in a bag, cans on a shelf, etc. Let your child count his or her own way. This might be by ones, twos, fives, or tens. When your child is finished counting, ask: *Can you think of another way to count these?*

Sincerely,

Mrs. Saxon

Your Child's Teacher

Menu Math

Dear ___Parent___,

Think about the ways you use math in a day and you'll see how useful math skills are in everyday life. Not surprisingly, learning how to add, subtract, and use other math skills is most meaningful to children in real-life situations. The next time you're relaxing at a restaurant or browsing a take-out menu, try these skill-building activities.

Menu Math

Have your child look at a menu. Ask questions that invite your child to explore numbers and work with addition and subtraction skills.

⊙ How many twos (or any other number) can you find before I count to ten?

⊙ Can you find a nine next to a five (or any other set of numbers) before I count to ten?

⊙ How many menu items on this menu cost $4.00?

⊙ How many menu items on this page cost more than $4.00?

⊙ How many menu items on this page cost between $4 and $7?

⊙ How many menu items cost less than $10?

⊙ How many menu items on this page cost more than $10?

⊙ Can I get anything for less than $1?

⊙ If I have $15 dollars, can I order [name several menu items]?

⊙ If I order [name several menu items], will my bill be more or less than $20?

Appetizers

| Nachos with salsa | $1.50 |
| Stuffed jalapeños | $2.00 |

Salads

| Salad bar (with dinner) | $1.95 |
| Salad bar only | $5.00 |

House Specials

Cheese enchiladas	$5.00
Beef enchiladas	$5.50
Chicken enchiladas	$5.50
Bean burritos	$4.00

Pizza

| Large | $6.50 |
| Small | $4.00 |

Side Dishes

| Rice | $1.00 |
| Refried beans | $2.00 |

Desserts

Flan	$1.95
Fried ice cream	$2.50
Fresh fruit	$2.00

Beverages

Cola	$1.00
Frozen fruitee	$2.00
Milk	$1.00
Iced tea	$1.00
Juice	$1.25

Sincerely,

Mrs. Sayon

Your Child's Teacher

Math Every Day

Dear _____,

Think about how often you use math every day—when you compare prices of two brands of dog food, when you leave a tip, when you cut a recipe in half. Your child needs math skills too—for example, to figure out how many pieces he or she gets when dividing a bag of candy with a friend or how many weeks' allowance it will take to save up for a new toy. Try these activities to strengthen your child's math skills.

One for You, One for Me

Look for items around the house for your child to divide equally among family members. For example, if you've got a basket of strawberries, how many can each person have? Encourage your child to guess first, then devise a way to find out. Your child can try the same thing when having a pretend party for stuffed animals. Given a bunch of grapes, how many will each guest get?

Cabinet Math

Open your kitchen cupboard doors for shelves full of math problems.

◎ Let your child line up cereal boxes by weight. Which box weighs most? Least?

◎ How much does a can of soup (or anything else) cost? About how much would two cans cost?

◎ Give your child a sum of pretend money (say $5) and ask him or her to "go shopping" in the cupboard. What things can he or she "buy" without going over?

◎ Give your child a box of noodles. Check to see how many servings are in the box. Ask: *Is one box enough for our family? How many boxes would we need to feed [fill in number] people?*

Play Restaurant

Children love to play restaurant. Give your child a pad of paper and pencil and let him or her "take orders" at a family meal. Post a "menu" that includes simple prices. Have your child total each order. How much are the orders all together?

Sincerely,

_____

Your Child's Teacher

Making Sense of Numbers

Dear _____ ,

Your child's experiences with math are helping him or her develop number concepts. This includes identifying quantities (how much) and discovering relationships between numbers. For example, your child might recognize that 7 + 3 and 2 + 8 both add up to 10. Or, your child might know by looking at a set of numbers, such as 4, 5, and 6, that the sum will be more or less than 10. Strengthen your child's understanding of numbers with these ideas.

Hidden Objects

Hold some small objects, such as marbles, in one hand. Let your child count them. While your child closes his or her eyes, put some of the objects under a bowl. Have your child look at the remaining objects. Ask: *How many did I hide under the bowl?*

More or Less?

Exercise your child's estimation skills with your phone number. Ask your child to guess whether the numbers in your phone number will add up to less than or more than 20. Have your child explain his or her answer, then add the numbers to find out. Now, have your child randomly choose another number in the phone book. Ask the same question. Have your child explain his or her answer, then add the numbers to find out.

Coins Add Up

Give your child an assortment of pennies, nickels, and dimes. Ask your child to show you how many ways there are to make the coins add up to some amount, such as 50 cents.

Sincerely,

_____

Your Child's Teacher

Numbers in the News

Dear _____,

Newspapers are full of real-life math, and there are lots of interesting ways you can use them to help your child build math skills.

Weather Report

Take a look at the weather section of your local paper. Find the high and low temperatures for the day. Look at the national summary for the highest and lowest temperatures of the day. How much higher and lower were they than where you live? Look at the five-day forecast. Let your child use the pictures to give a weather report.

Tip

You can also find weather information on the Internet at **www.accuweather.com**.

Be a Better Shopper

Build consumer skills with coupons your child clips from the paper. Have your child sort out the ones for foods and other items your family uses. Together, find out how much you can save by using them.

Scoreboard

Look at the sports section of the paper for more math fun. Find the statistics for a favorite sport. Compare scores and other information. Look at scheduling information on TV or radio sports programs. Can your child tell what times the shows are on? What other information is provided?

Sincerely,

_____

Your Child's Teacher

A World of Math

Dear _Parents_ ,

You can reinforce math skills and concepts at just about any time of the day. Take first thing in the morning. There's the time your child wakes up, the shape of the soap and washcloth he or she uses, the amount of cereal in a serving, the number of minutes until the bus comes… Walks are another wonderful opportunity to find math in the real world. From numbers on buildings to shapes of street signs and sets of wheels on bikes, cars, and buses, math is everywhere. Try these activities with your child to build math into your time together.

Street Math

The next time you take a walk with your child, take a look at street addresses. Notice the numbers on one side. Compare them to the numbers on the other side. Invite your child to tell why he or she thinks street addresses are numbered this way.

Pattern Detectives

Take a look around. There are patterns almost everywhere—in the way leaves grow on a branch, the way boards are used to build a fence, the way the colors change on a stoplight. Recognizing patterns helps your child organize information, make connections, and develop reasoning skills. When you take a walk, or while you're waiting for a bus, look for patterns together. Describe them!

I Spy Shapes

Investigating shapes is one of the ways your child learns about geometry. Play "I Spy Shapes" to learn more. Start by saying "I spy a… (name a shape you see—for example, a square). Have your child name something he or she sees that has that shape. Switch places: Your child names a shape and you find the object.

Sincerely,

Mrs. Saxon

Your Child's Teacher

Pick a Pattern

Dear **Parents**,

Have you ever seen your child hop down a stone walk, being ever so careful to step only on every so many stones? That's a pattern in action! When your child creates or discovers patterns, he or she is exploring mathematical relationships. Looking for patterns can help your child make sense of mathematical problems. For example, skip counting by tens creates the pattern 10, 20, 30, 40, 50, and so on. Your child can use this understanding to solve related math problems such as, "If one lollipop costs 10 cents, how much will five cost?"

Moving Patterns

When you take a walk with your child (or just head out to the bus stop), take turns making patterns for the other to replicate. For example, hop on one foot twice, then hop on both feet three times. Repeat to make a pattern.

Guess My Pattern

Give your child an assortment of dried pasta shapes, stickers, or pieces of cereal. Let him or her start a pattern with the pieces. Add on to your child's pattern, then switch places: You make a pattern for your child to finish.

Number Connections

Look for opportunities for your child to skip count. Socks to be sorted, shoes in a line, mittens in a basket, legs on chairs, panes of a window…they're all invitations to count by twos, fours, tens, or some other number. As your child counts, help him or her discover patterns or regularities. For example, your child may not be able to count by fours, but he or she may discover that the chairs at the table have four legs each.

Sincerely,

Mrs. Saxon

Your Child's Teacher

Learning About Measurement

Dear _____,

Think about the measurements people take in everyday life. People measure windows to buy shades. They measure feet to fit shoes. They measure flour and milk to bake cakes. Sometimes measurements need to be accurate. Sometimes they can be inexact. People estimate the length of ribbon needed to tie up a gift. They sprinkle in approximately the tablespoon of herbs called for in a recipe. Use the following activities at home to strengthen your child's measuring skills.

About the Same

Have your child use his or her hand as a measuring tool. How many things are about the same size as your child's open hand? How many hands long is the couch? How many hands wide is the front door?

Longer, Shorter

Give your child a length of string. Invite your child to find things that are longer than the string and shorter than the string. Can your child find something that is the same length as the string?

How Tall? How Long? How Wide?

A tape measure makes a surprisingly fun toy. Let your child use one to take measurements around the house. Offer prompts, such as: *How tall is the tallest part of your bed? How long is your dog? How wide is the refrigerator?* Let your child keep going, sharing his or her findings with you.

Sincerely,

_____

Your Child's Teacher

Thinking Mathematically

Dear _____ ,

Your child uses thinking skills to solve problems every day. In a game of checkers, for example, your child may wonder aloud about a move: "I could move there, but I might get jumped." "If I jump you, you can double-jump me." To solve the addition problem 5 + 10, your child might think, "Hmmm, I know that 5 plus 5 equals 10. So this is like three fives. 5, 10, 15...5 + 10 is 15!" This kind of thinking is an example of logical reasoning, something that comes into play not only in mathematics, but in many areas of life. Strengthen your child's logical reasoning skills with these activities.

Take Away

Set out 13 objects. These can be playing cards, pennies, marbles...almost any object will do. Take turns taking away either one or two objects. The object of the game is to make the other player take the last object.

What's the Same?

Welcome your child to the breakfast table with an assortment of objects that have something in common. Invite your child to figure out how the objects are alike.

The pancakes are to eat, but nothing else is . . . The plate and coaster are for setting things on, but the others aren't . . . **I** know! They're all **ROUND!**

Math Challenge

Give your child an interesting math question to think through each day or week. For example, if you're making pancakes, ask: *If we mix one cup of flour with one cup of milk, will the mixture equal two cups?* Or: *How could you find out how much our cat weighs if it won't sit still on the scale?* Encourage your child to think through possible answers aloud.

Sincerely,

_____

Your Child's Teacher

Fraction Fun

Dear _____ ,

Your child began learning about fractions long before he or she started school. The milk your child puts on breakfast cereal may come from a half-gallon carton. You may cut apples in quarters or bagels in half. At bath time, you may fill the tub halfway. Your child may say he or she is 6 1/2 years old! Here are some ways you can further your child's experiences with fractions.

Shopping for Fractions

Look for fractions at the grocery store together. For example, if you're buying produce, let your child weigh it. Ask: *Do we have more or less than half a pound?* Talk about what fractions mean: *How many half-gallon cartons of milk equal a one-gallon jug?*

Eating Fractions

Look for fractions at a meal or snack. For example, before your child eats a section of an orange, count the pieces together. Ask: *If you eat one piece, how many will be left?* Ask for an orange section using a fraction. (*Can I have one-eighth of your orange?*)

Measuring Fractions

Using measuring cups and spoons is a great way to explore simple fractions. Here's an easy no-cook recipe for play clay you can mix up together.

Sincerely,

_____

Your Child's Teacher

Play Clay

1 1/2 cups flour
1/2 cup salt
1/2 cup water

1/4 cup vegetable oil
food coloring

Mix flour and salt together. Add water and oil. Knead the dough until smooth. Divide into pieces and add food coloring as desired. Play with the clay to learn more about fractions. Make a clay quesadilla; cut it into eight pieces. Make a clay cookie. Divide it in half. Store clay in a plastic bag in the refrigerator when not in use.

Name _____

Date _____

Ask Me About Science

I did a science experiment in school today. Ask me to tell you about it!

Here's a picture of my experiment.

Name _____

Date _____

Ask Me About Science

I wrote in my science journal today. Ask me to tell you about my ideas.

Here's a picture about my journal entry.

Name _____

Date _____

Ask Me About Science

In science today I learned about _____
_____.

Ask me to tell you more.

Here's a picture that shows what I learned.

Name _____

Date _____

Ask Me About Science

We read a book about science today.
Title: _____
_____

Ask me to tell you about it!

Here's a picture about the book.

Name _____ Date _____

Ask Me About Science

I learned some new science words today.

_____

_____

_____

Ask me to tell you about them!

- -

Name _____

Date _____

Ask Me About Science

_____

_____

_____

_____

_____

Here's a picture about_____.

61

Think Like a Scientist

Dear _____ ,

Children are born scientists. Their many questions and observations about the world around them are just one sign of this. Children are mesmerized by bugs, by sprouting seeds, by the wind that moves their pinwheels, by snow falling, by puddles disappearing, by their shadows, and more. You can encourage your child's natural interest in science by asking questions yourself. "Correct" answers are not required! The goal is to encourage your child's curiosity about the world. Here's a starter list of questions you can ask to encourage your child's thinking skills.

- Where do you think rain comes from? (clouds, snow, etc.)
- What do you think makes birds fly?
- Why do you think the leaves on the trees move?
- Where do you think wind comes from?
- What do you think makes the sky blue?
- (on a cloudy day) Where do you think the sun is today?
- Why do you think the moon seems to change shape?
- Why do you think water turns to ice in the freezer?

- Why do you think ice cream melts when it's not in the freezer?
- What do you think happens to ice when we take it out of the freezer?
- Why do you think leaves change color?
- Why do you think all leaves are not the same?
- What do you think makes seeds grow into plants?
- How do you think your body uses the food you eat?
- How do you think cookie batter turns into cookies?

Sincerely,

_____

Your Child's Teacher

Science and Play

Dear _____ ,

Encouraging your child's interest in science doesn't necessarily mean buying microscopes and fancy kits. The everyday activities children most enjoy are filled with opportunities to build science skills and concepts. Here are just a few of the playful ways your child can do science at home.

Science at the Sink

Does your child ever ask to wash dishes? This activity is loaded with built-in science investigations. Remove any unsafe objects, such as knives and breakable items. Place a towel on the floor, and then let your child go to work. As your child plays, ask questions such as: *Where do you think the bubbles come from? How do you think they get their shape? If a dish floats, how can you make it sink? Do you think a tall container holds more or less water than other containers? How can you test this? Where do you think the water in the sink comes from? Where do you think water goes when it leaves the sink?*

Building With Blocks

Blocks are an endless source of science experimentation—from trying to find the best way to get a heavy box of blocks from one place to another to testing different bases to find out which combination of blocks at the bottom will result in the tallest tower. As your child plays, ask questions such as: *Which blocks do you think make the best base for a tall tower? How could you test that idea?*

Combining Colors

When your child paints, offer paper, assorted paint colors, and brushes. Then stay out of the way! What will happen? Your child will very likely mix colors—maybe not in combinations you'd choose. But in the process, your child will make discoveries about colors. Follow up by asking questions, such as: *What colors did you mix to make this color? What do you think would happen if you added a new color?*

Sincerely,

_____

Your Child's Teacher

Strengthening Observation Skills

Dear _____,

Whether you live on a city block or in the country, walks are a way to reinforce a range of science skills that your child will use in class and beyond. One of those skills is *observing*. Observing is the way your child uses his or her senses to notice details. An example of this is noticing patterns and colors in a butterfly's wings (sight), or noticing the texture of a tree's bark (touch). Here are three walks you and your child can take to strengthen observation skills.

We're All Ears!

Take a listening walk together. Ask your child to be very quiet for a minute or two. After the walk, talk about the things you both heard.

Rainbow Hunt

Challenge your child to spot something on your walk for each color of the rainbow: red, orange, yellow, green, blue, and purple. (Purple combines indigo and violet, the last two colors of the spectrum.) Invite your child to create a picture of the walk.

Please Touch!

From early on, the sense of touch plays an important role for children in discovering their world. Take a "Please Touch!" walk, inviting your child to find things that are smooth, soft, bumpy, rough, slippery, furry, and so on.

Sincerely,

_____

Your Child's Teacher

Strengthening Classification Skills

Dear _____,

Sorting comes naturally to children. They sort blocks by shapes. They sort collections of rocks, shells, and marbles. They're experts at sorting foods, too: foods I like, foods I don't like. When children sort, they use a science skill called *classification*. Classification is simply sorting and grouping objects according to some attribute. In science, an example of classifying is grouping animals according to a common attribute. Your child might recognize, for example, that birds have wings. Animals that do not have wings, therefore, do not belong in this group. You can strengthen this skill at home by setting up sorting games.

Junk Drawer Sort

Take any unsafe objects out of your "junk drawer." Then let your child have a go at it. (You can purchase drawer trays with dividers at kitchen stores. Ice cube trays and small boxes make handy holders, too.) Have your child first sort the objects on a large surface, then put them away. Rubber bands, coins, paper clips, spare keys, and hardware are just a few of the groups your child might make.

What's for Dinner?

Gather a pile of coupons for cereal, frozen vegetables, crackers, and other foods. Invite your child to sort the coupons—for example, *foods I like, foods I don't like*. Discuss your child's sorting rules. Let your child re-sort them, this time according to your sorting rules.

Sock Sort

Let your child sort clean socks—starting by gathering socks in a pile, then sorting the ones that belong to him or her. From there, your child can look for pairs. Encourage your child to notice details about the socks as he or she sorts.

Sincerely,

_____

Your Child's Teacher

Strengthening Communication Skills

Dear _____ ,

When your child shares information by writing, speaking, drawing, or some other way (such as making a graph), he or she is communicating in the same ways scientists do. Following are strategies for strengthening your child's communication skills.

Tell Me More

When you ask, "What did you do today?" do you sometimes get "Nothing" for an answer? Getting a child to use his or her communication skills isn't always easy. Look for the right moment to encourage your child's comments about something. When your child gets dressed in the morning, for example, you might look out the window together and ask: *What clothes do you think you'll want to wear today? Why?* And when you want to know about your child's day, ask open-ended questions with a bit of direction, such as, *What was the best/funniest/worst part about your day today?*

My Turn, Your Turn

Make a small blank book by stapling plain paper together. Take turns writing about what you see in the world around you. For example, when it's your turn, you might write about a bird you saw. Record comments or questions about each other's entries in the book, too. Your child will look forward to these communications with you.

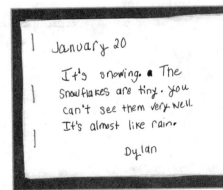

Watch Me!

Let your child observe the ways you communicate, whether it's memos from work, conversations, faxes and e-mails, diagrams you make, phone messages you leave, and so on. Explain the purpose of each—to share information with others. Help your child understand the various reasons for different communications. Ask your child to share some of the ways he or she communicates each day.

Sincerely,

_____

Your Child's Teacher

Strengthening Measurement Skills

Dear _____,

When your child puts his or her foot next to yours to see whose is bigger, or pours juice from one cup to another to "see if it will fit," there's science going on. Measuring is a science and math skill your child uses to solve problems. Your child can use conventional tools, such as rulers, to measure size. Your child can also measure with other tools, such as a string, a foot, or an arm span. You can support this skill at home with these activities.

Size Order

Let your child physically arrange people (and pets) in the family according to size order (shortest to tallest or tallest to shortest). Ask your child where family members who are not present (such as a grandmother) might go in the order. Encourage your child to explain his or her measuring methods.

Shoelace Measure

Give your child a shoelace. Ask: *What can you measure with this?* Watch as your child measures everything from you to the walls in a room. Together, make comparisons about the measurements—for example, *What things are [taller, shorter, longer, etc.] than your string?*

How Much Does It Hold?

While your child is helping out with the dishes some evening, invite him or her to experiment with how much water different containers hold. Let your child pour water from one to another to predict and discover which containers hold the same amount, more, or less. Talk about shape: *Does a taller container always hold more?*

Sincerely,

_____

Your Child's Teacher

Strengthening Prediction Skills

Dear _____,

When your child guesses that it's going to rain today, or that a bike that has been in the garage all winter will need air in the tires, he or she is using predicting skills. By using observations, and what he or she already knows, your child can learn to make more accurate predictions. Predicting is one of the science skills your child uses to understand the world. To support your child in developing predicting skills, try these activities.

The Moon Makes a Pattern

The moon's phases follow a predictable pattern. Spend time with your child observing the moon. Record what you see each night. (You can also get this information from the weather section of the newspaper.) After a few days, ask your child to look at the drawings and guess what shape he or she will see the next night.

| New | Waxing crescent | First quarter | Waxing gibbous | Full | Waning gibbous | Last quarter | Waning crescent |

Outside Scientists

Use the weather conditions each day as a source of predicting activities. For example, after a rain, go outside and look at puddles. Ask your child: *What do you think will happen to this puddle? How long do you think it will take to evaporate (dry up)?* Keep track of the puddle as it disappears. Let your child modify his or her prediction along the way.

What Will We See?

When you take a walk with your child, start by asking: *What do you think we'll see?* Invite your child to make predictions, then take a walk together to find out.

Sincerely,

_____

Your Child's Teacher

Strengthening Comparing Skills

Dear _____,

Discovering the ways things are alike and different is one of the ways children develop an understanding of their world. For example, by comparing an ant with a beetle, your child can discover that both have the same number of legs (six). This may be the beginning of your child's understanding that insects all have six legs. Work on comparing skills at home with these activities.

What Fits?

Form a large circle with string. Gather a variety of objects, some of which have something in common. Place several objects that are alike in some way in the circle. Invite your child to find another object that belongs in the circle. For example, you might place things that are smaller than a quarter in the circle. Anything larger would stay outside the circle.

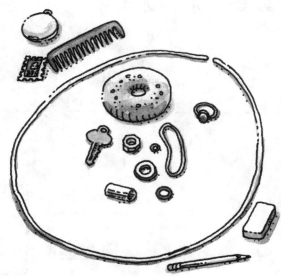

We Are Alike, We Are Different

Look for everyday ways to make comparisons in the world around you.

◎ Compare your breakfast with your child's. How is it alike? How is it different?

◎ Compare what you and your child are wearing. How are your clothes alike? How are they different?

◎ Compare your day with your child's. In what ways were your days similar? In what ways were they different?

Sincerely,

_____

Your Child's Teacher

Name _____

Date _____

Ask Me About Our Community

Today I learned something about our community. Ask me to tell you more.

Here's a picture of something in **our community**.

Name _____

Date _____

Ask Me About History

Today I learned about this special person:

_____.

Ask me to tell you about him or her.

Here's a picture of

_____.

Name _____

Date _____

Ask Me About the World

Today I learned about a new place. Ask me to tell you about it!

Here's a picture of the place.

- -

Name _____

Date _____

Ask Me About Getting Along

Today I learned about solving problems with friends. Ask me to tell you about it!

Here's a picture of me and a friend.

Getting Along

Dear _____ ,

Your child is learning about groups. Our class is a group. Your child's family is a group. So is our community. There are many other kinds of groups people belong to, including different cultures. Part of learning about the groups to which people belong is learning about getting along. Sometimes there are rules that help people get along. Sometimes people need to learn their own strategies for getting along. Help your child develop skills for getting along with these activities.

Read About It

Books are a wonderful way to teach your child some of life's lessons, including how to get along with others. Some suggestions follow.

◎ *Smoky Night* by Eve Bunting (Harcourt Brace, 1994). This evocative story shows conflict in a community and what happens to bring people together.

◎ *No Fighting, No Biting!* by Else Holmelund Minarik (HarperCollins, 1978). Willy and Rosa behave a bit like the quarreling alligators in a story their cousin reads to them.

◎ *I'll Fix Anthony* by Judith Viorst (Aladdin, 1969). When the brothers in this book have trouble getting along, let your child suggest ways to handle the situation.

Problems and Solutions

What are some common problems at home? Do siblings argue over TV shows? Do household chores go undone? Work together to find solutions—for example, at a family meeting. Whatever the problem, encourage family members to keep these guidelines in mind.

◎ Use quiet voices to encourage a calm discussion.

◎ Consider one another's viewpoints as you discuss problems and solutions.

◎ Let speakers finish their thoughts uninterrupted.

Before and After

Invite your child to draw a "before" picture that represents a problem in your household. After working out a solution and trying it for a week or so, ask your child to draw an "after" picture. Have your child tell you about each picture.

Sincerely,

_____

Your Child's Teacher

Improving Communication Skills

Dear _____ ,

"You said I could watch TV when my homework was finished!" "I meant if you finished earlier. It's bedtime now." How often do you and your child have a miscommunication like this? Effective communication is a lifelong skill that relies on communicating clearly and being understood. Here are some activities for strengthening your child's communication skills.

Did You Hear Me?

"You can watch TV after your homework is finished—as long as it's finished before dinner." "You mean I can't watch TV if I'm not done by dinner?" Paraphrasing—repeating what someone said in your own words—is a great way to improve communication skills. It lets the listener know if what he or she heard is what the speaker meant to communicate. Practice paraphrasing with your child. Try these topics for starters:

◎ Things I like about my friends.

◎ Things my friends do that make me mad.

Start by paraphrasing what your child says. Then switch places and let your child paraphrase what you say.

Picture This

Have your child draw a simple picture but not show it to you. Then have your child tell you, using words only, how to make the same picture. Draw the picture and set it aside. Repeat the activity, having your child make a new picture. This time your child can use words and gestures to explain how to make the picture. Try the activity a third time. This time, your child can use words and gestures, as well as answer questions from you, to describe how to make the picture. Which way of communicating worked best?

Sincerely,

_____

Your Child's Teacher

The World Around Us

Dear _____ ,

"How long 'til we get there?" This common question, asked by just about every child taking a trip lasting any longer than five minutes, is an invitation to explore geography. Whether you're taking a trip to the grocery store or traveling across the country, you can build geography into the experience with these activities.

Scavenger Hunt

Before a trip, prepare a scavenger hunt for your child. List ten things your child can look for along the way. (Adapt the sample scavenger hunt here to reflect your geographic area.) Give your child a clipboard to hold the paper and a pencil for recording what he or she finds.

Scavenger Hunt
Can you find:
1. a body of water
2. a bridge
3. someone fishing
4. children playing
5. a place for animals to live
6. a farm
7. a business
8. two different kinds of trees
9. a train
10. a hill or mountain

Minutes and Miles

Make time fly with this travel game. Have everyone traveling with you make a guess: *How many minutes or miles will it be until we see a [river, farm, etc.]?* Let everyone take a guess, then start the clock (or odometer). Take turns deciding what to look for and keeping track of the time.

World Explorers

Take a blow-up globe along on a trip. (These are beach-ball-like globes available in many toy and discount stores.) Ask your child questions that invite him or her to explore the world. For example: *What countries border our country? What countries border [any other country]? Can you find an island? What is its name?* Learn more about other places by displaying a map in the house. Use it to locate places family members live or travel. (*Grandma is visiting your Aunt Kim in California. Let's see where that is.*)

Sincerely,

_____

Your Child's Teacher

Jobs People Do

Dear _____ ,

Learning about jobs helps your child understand the goods and services workers provide. Exploring jobs is also an opportunity to introduce the concept of *needs and wants*. Expand your child's understanding of these concepts with these activities.

What's My Job?

Play a guessing game. Describe a job for your child, without naming the job. Let your child guess what it is. For example: *Animals come to see this person when they're sick. Sometimes they come to see this person when they're well, too. They might need a shot or a checkup. What's this person's job?*

Classified Information

For some real-life reading, investigate jobs in the classified section of the newspaper. Read them with your child. Ask: *What does a person have to be able to do for this job? How do you think a person who can do this job learned these skills? Does a person who works at this job provide goods or services? Are these goods or services things people* need *or* want?

Ask Me!

Encourage your child to ask grown-up friends and family members about the jobs they do. Questions to ask include: *What is your job? Where do you do your job? Does anyone work with you? Why did you pick this job? What goods or services does your work provide? Do people get paid at this job or do they volunteer?*

Sincerely,

_____

Your Child's Teacher

Community News

Dear _____,

As part of an exploration of our community, your child is learning about neighborhoods, homes, maps, and more. Here are some activities for reinforcing related concepts at home.

Your Home and Beyond

Strengthen basic map skills by making a simple map with your child. Ask your child to draw a picture of your home in the center of a sheet of paper. Ask your child to draw what is in front of your home, behind your home, to the left, and to the right. Have your child draw these things on the map. Hang it up!

Where Am I?

Play a guessing game with your child to learn more about your community. Think of a place in the community. Give one clue about its identity. Let your child guess what it is. Give additional clues, one at a time, until your child guesses the place. Then let your child give you clues about another place in the community.

Who's Who?

Help your child learn about people in your community. Look at the metro section of your local paper together. Ask your child: *Can you find a story about someone in our community?* Your child might see stories about volunteers, students involved in a special project, and so on. Discuss the kinds of things people in a community do. Invite your child to tell you about other people in the community he or she knows.

Sincerely,

_____

Your Child's Teacher

Time Lines Tell Stories

Dear _____,

Working with time lines helps your child develop an understanding of events in history. Here are some activities to strengthen your child's time line skills and sense of personal history. This will help build a foundation for an understanding of people, events, inventions, and so on in the history of other time periods.

Family Photos

One of the best ways to help your child develop a sense of history is to look at family photos together. Pull out a stack of photos and select a dozen or so from different times in your child's life. Together with your child, place the photos in chronological order. As you do, share stories about what you see in the photos.

Family Time Line

Make a family time line. Draw a horizontal line on a large sheet of paper. At the far left, write the year your family began. At regular intervals, mark off each additional year. Together, fill in memorable events in your family's history—for example, the birth of children, moves, trips, and so on.

1991	1992	1993	1994	1995	1996
Louise met Sharif at a party	They got married	They got Jake at the dog shelter	Mom got pregnant	I was born in September	Dad went to Egypt

Personal Time Line

Using the same format as the Family Time Line, guide your child in making a personal time line. Help your child with events from the first few years. Let your child use words or pictures to tell about events. Encourage your child to tell you about the events included in the time line, starting with the first event.

Sincerely,

_____

Your Child's Teacher

Alike and Different

Dear _____,

Your child is learning about the many kinds of people that make up our schools, communities, nation, and world. In the process, your child will learn how he or she is alike and different from other people. This understanding can help your child develop a sense of connectedness to the world and respect for the people in it.

Our Family

What are some ways your child is like other members of the family? What are some ways your child is different? For example, maybe you and your child both have curly hair. But maybe you like pineapple on your pizza and your child prefers pepperoni. Make similar comparisons among family members. Help your child see that he or she can be both like and different from another person.

In or Out?

Has your child ever felt *excluded* from a group of friends? How about *included*? Helping children understand what both inclusion and exclusion feel like helps them develop empathy—a quality that will help them be sensitive to other people's feelings and fair in their actions. Children's books can help you develop this quality in your child. Some wonderful titles follow. Ask your school or public librarian for more.

- *Chrysanthemum* by Kevin Henkes (Greenwillow, 1991). A young girl's classmates exclude her because of her name—it's *soooo* long *and* it's the name of a flower.

- *Oliver Button Is a Sissy* by Tomie de Paola (Harcourt Brace, 1979). A boy is teased because he would rather dance, read, and paint than play ball.

- *Amazing Grace* by Mary Hoffman (Dial, 1996). A young girl's peers try to exclude her from the role of Peter in a school production of *Peter Pan* for two reasons: she is a girl and she is African American.

- *Be Good to Eddie Lee* by Virginia Fleming (Putnam, 1993). Children discover a friend in Eddie Lee, a boy with Down's syndrome.

Sincerely,

_____

Your Child's Teacher

Making Choices

Dear _____ ,

Your child is learning that people vote to make choices about schools, towns, states, and their country. Here's how you can help your child learn more about voting.

Make a Family Ballot Box

Bring the vote to your family by making a ballot box. Let your child decorate a shoebox. Cut a slit in the cover. Find a spot for the ballot box and place slips of paper and a pencil next to it. Brainstorm things that your family can vote on. Following are some ideas.

- Vote for family activities. Whether you have regular family time set aside each week or plan events as schedules allow, let family members suggest activities, then vote on them.

- Vote for dinner choices. At least once a week, or as your meal planning allows, offer a choice for dinner and take a vote.

- Vote for solutions to problems. Identify problems in the family—for example, arguing over which TV show to watch or how often rooms need to be cleaned. Let everyone suggest a solution, then take a vote.

- Vote on favorite books or songs or movies. Invite each person to give reasons for nominations before voting.

- Vote on names for a new pet.

- Vote on when things happen. For example, will the family do chores before or after a bike ride?

Sincerely,

_____

Your Child's Teacher

Celebrating Special Days

Dear _____ ,

Your child is learning about special days and celebrations. What special days does your family celebrate? Help your child learn more about the significance of special days with these activities.

Mark Your Calendars

Make a list of special days. Let your child find each day on the calendar and draw a picture on the calendar to symbolize it. Every so often, invite your child to guess when the next holiday is. Have your child find it on the calendar and count the days until it arrives.

Tell Holiday Stories

Families celebrate special days in different ways. What are some of your family's holiday traditions? Share stories with your child about holidays. Talk about what the holidays meant to you as a child and what they mean now. You might include traditional holiday foods, decorations, and so on. Then let your child tell you about his or her favorite holiday.

Making Memories

Place pocket folders in a binder to make a book about family traditions. On each folder, write the name of a holiday your family celebrates. Fill the folder pockets with recipes, poems, activities, stories, and other materials you can pull out when each holiday comes around. Let your child add pictures and stories about the holidays to the folders. You'll enjoy revisiting these together each year.

Sincerely,

_____

Your Child's Teacher